M000086119

SEVEN
SAYINGS
One
FRIDAY

Kenn Filkins

COLLEGE PRESS
PUBLISHING COMPANY
Joplin, Missouri

International Standard Book Number 0-89900-707-4

CONTENTS

STUDIES FOR SMALL GROUPS

Welcome to the *Studies for Small Groups* series from College Press, which is designed for simplicity of use while giving insight into important issues of the Christian life. Some volumes in this series examine a passage of Scripture for the day-to-day lessons we can learn from it. Others are topical studies, using a wide range of Scripture resources. The present study falls somewhat in between, as it covers a single set of Scriptures, the Gospel accounts of the crucifixion of Jesus.

A number of possible uses could be made of this study. Because there are a limited number of lessons, the format is ideal for new or potential Christians who can begin the study without feeling that they are tied into an overly long commitment. It could also be used for one or two months of weekly studies by a home Bible study group. The series is suitable for individual as well as group study.

Of course, any study is only as good as the effort you put into it. The group leader should study each lesson carefully before the group study session, and if possible, come up with additional Scriptures and other supporting material. Although study questions are provided for each lesson, it would also be helpful if the leader can add his or her own questions.

Neither is it necessary to complete a full lesson in one class period. If the discussion is going well, don't feel that you have to cut it off to fit time constraints, as long as the discussion is related to the topic and not off on side issues.

College Press is happy to present this new eight lesson study called *Seven Sayings One Friday*. At no time are a person's most profound motives and interests more evident than as death approaches. Jesus made seven statements from the cross that have been recorded for our benefit. As we try to imitate Him, we can learn from the types of things that held His attention while He hung dying.

SEVEN SAYINGS ONE FRIDAY

Have you ever wondered what it would be like to experience Calvary that fateful Friday? Have you ever wondered what it felt like to see the nails, to hear the hammer ring, to look into Mary's eyes while you hear His accusers' jeers and the believers weep? Have you felt the tear of emotions that ripped everyone that Friday? Amidst the trauma, have you heard His strong, steady voice offering comfort and hope?

And His *voice* — that had held the Galilean multitudes spellbound, that spoke such tender words to the outcast and downtrodden, that whispered into a dead girl's ear moments before her face blushed with life — *that voice* of Christ at Calvary spoke seven statements which transformed some, tormented others, and touched all those present.

Those seven statements, as we will see in these lessons, reached out with forgiveness, tenderly cared for a mother's broken heart, showed His simple humanity and His sublime deity, proclaimed victory in the face of defeat, remembered a forgettable thief, and placed Himself — and all believers — in the hands of His Heavenly Father.

Won't you don your sandals and walk with us up the dusty streets of Jerusalem to a hill called Calvary? Won't you join us as we listen to the final words of Jesus? If you do, you won't come back the same. No one ever has . . .

1
O N E

CHRIST'S COURAGE AND COMPASSION AT CALVARY

As a refiner's fire forces the hidden dross to the surface of the gold, crisis and stress reveal our real character. Stress strips away the mask and façade to reveal our heart. Crucifixion was the greatest stress for the greatest person — Jesus Christ. His words reveal the seven most important topics of living and dying. Calvary reveals Christ's courage and compassion for mankind in a unique way. Through the crisis of Calvary we get a clear glimpse into Jesus' heart. He was under the greatest stress — suffering for crimes He did not commit, dying for a people who didn't care.

In times of crisis priorities become clearer. When someone's spouse is diagnosed with terminal cancer, the dent in the fender seems less significant. Families and friends always press to listen to the words of a dying loved one, then share those last words with others. Why? Because, the words of a dying person are those closest to their heart. Those who love them know that the end is near and any of these words can be their last. These final words are their heart cry. The sayings of Jesus from the Cross are His heart cry to us.

These seven sayings reveal Jesus' heart in a uniquely meaningful way and depict life's most important topics.

CHRIST'S PULPIT — THE CROSS

Crucifixion was the ultimate stress, so much so that it sounds trite to even mention the words stress and crucifixion together. Crucifixion is much too cruel and brutal to call it only a stress. *But the Cross was stressful and it was Christ's last pulpit from which He preached His last sermon — with just seven sayings.* His preparation for this sermon came at the hands of the prejudiced, brutal, callous soldiers.

Jesus endured trials before both the Jewish High Priests (Matthew 26:57 & John 18:13), Pilate (Matthew 27:13) and Herod (Luke 23:7) where all of His accusers perjured themselves. Following His trials came the beatings, the crown of thorns, the purple robe and the pounding He took from the hands of the Roman soldiers (Matthew 26:67,68). With a "cat of nine tails" whip with nine leather thongs tipped with jagged metal, the Romans scourged Jesus so badly that He could not even carry His own cross to Calvary. Simon of Cyrene carried it (Matthew 27:32).

Then came the act of crucifixion. Though the Romans did not invent crucifixion, they perfected it. *Crucifixion was the most cruel, merciless, torturous way to execute someone.* The Romans meant it to be. Once Jesus was laid on the cross, His arms were stretched out, soldiers held Him there. They never knew that they did not need to hold Him there. Nor did they know that they *could not* hold Him there, without His consent. Then one soldier pounded in the nail through His wrist between the two

> The Cross was Christ's last pulpit from which He preached His last sermon — with just seven sayings.

10

bones in His forearm. The Romans soldiers never drove nails in the middle of the hands; these tendons are not strong enough to hold a person's whole weight. Jesus' feet were laid one over the other and a nail was driven through them. The Romans did this so that the crucified person would linger longer on the cross as a public display. Some crucified persons lasted up to six days. As with Jesus the soldiers could give the prisoners drinks.

If the soldiers did not nail their feet, the crucified would die of suffocation in a matter of minutes. When a person was hung by his arms, his body weight pulled up his diaphragm and kept him from drawing his next breath. He died quickly. The Romans wanted the condemned to suffer as a public spectacle. If the Romans desired a quick death they beheaded them with a sword (Acts 12:2). Nailing the feet allowed the executed person to push himself up with his legs to take a breath and even talk. But soon the pain in his feet would become intense and he would fall back down on to his arms, until he needed another breath. That torturous cycle repeated itself again and again, hour after hour, day into day, until death finally came. The wounds the soldiers inflicted during crucifixion were *not* fatal wounds — they just held the person on the cross. What did the soldiers do that Friday night when the Jews wanted the crucified off the crosses before sundown? They took clubs and broke the legs of the two thieves, and minutes later they had suffocated to death.

Another humiliating aspect of crucifixion was nakedness. The Roman soldiers stripped the prisoners and hung them on the cross naked. The loincloths in all the pictures of Jesus are for our modesty; the Romans were not so kind at Calvary. Jesus hung naked before both

His mother and His Heavenly Father. The Romans stripped the condemned naked and without inflicting a fatal wound hung them in the sun for days with a centurion and four soldiers as guards. This torture, humiliation, and cruelty was as a testimony to the occupied country, *Don't do what this person did unless you want the same!* Their method was effective.

"TAKE UP YOUR CROSS"

We respond so differently today, than the crowd along the Sea of Galilee when Jesus uttered this challenge, "Take up his cross daily and follow Me" (Luke 9:23). *We respond by imagining the beautiful wooden cross on the steeple or in the church,* or we think of the beautiful selection of golden and silver crosses available at the Christian bookstore. But Jesus' audience had never sung our cherished hymn, "The Old Rugged Cross." The words of Jesus stung like a dagger, and a chill swept over them as they visualized the Roman soldiers stripping prisoners, driving in the nails and hanging criminals naked in the sun for all to see, to spit on and to despise.

Jesus' audience knew that the crucified had no hidden agendas, could not turn back, and were completely vulnerable. And Christ commanded them — and us — to love as He loved at Calvary. "My command is this: Love each other as I have loved you. Greater love has no one than this, that he lay down his life for his friends" (John 15:12,13). In contrast to the convenient "feel good" love of today's culture, Jesus modeled that true love can mean pain, struggle and self-sacrifice. But that Friday's love which appeared defeated was victorious on Sunday. "Whoever finds his life will lose it, and whoever loses his

> We imagine the beautiful wooden cross on the steeple or in the church.

12

life for my sake will find it" (Matthew 10:39).

Part of the mystery of Calvary is that Christ had the power to stop it at any time.

LOVE IS A CHOICE

Part of the mystery of Calvary is that Christ had the power to stop it at any time. He had the power to stop those who beat Him, tortured Him and crucified Him.

"The reason my Father loves me is that I lay down my life — only to take it up again. No one takes it from me, but I lay it down of my own accord. I have authority to lay it down and authority to take it up again. This command I received from my Father" (John 10:17–18).

Surely this Jesus Who, with just the sound of His voice, took a dead man and made him alive, could take a live man and make him dead. That makes His endurance of the mocking trials, the savage beatings, and the unbearable crucifixion even more amazing. He could have stopped it at any time. So it was not the nails that held Jesus to the cross. It was love.

Where could Jesus get such self-control in a time of public ridicule? Where did His reserve of courage and compassion come from? What was the source of His hidden strength?

HIS HIDDEN STRENGTH

Public battles are always won during private moments of commitment. The public Battle of Calvary was with the cursing mob, the jeering of His enemies, the indifference of the torturers, the shame of the family, the weeping of the distraught, the despair of His mother and hopelessness of His faithful followers. But that Battle was won not in the scorching morning sun; it was won in a cool, quiet, solitary *garden* (Luke 22:39–46).

13

There Jesus struggled with the battle to come and said, "Father, if you are willing, take this cup from me; yet not my will, but yours be done" (Luke 22:42). And drops of sweat like blood trickled down His brow (Luke 23:44). It was not an easy decision but He won the battle when He prayed, "yet not My will, but Yours be done." Jesus had no divided heart as He went through the trials, beatings, and His crucifixion. In the midst of suffering He never wondered if He should continue, or why He must bear this cup of suffering. He endured. He forgave. He loved. He rescued. Satan could not sway Him because after Gethsemane His heart was undivided. He was committed in love to do the right thing, the tough thing . . . God's will. The courage and compassion of Calvary came from the commitment of Gethsemane.

Early in the morning, my wife and I walk three to four miles a few days a week. We have different courses with different difficulties. If we do not *predetermine* how long a course and how hard a course before we begin, it is easy and very tempting to go the easy way or to take a shortcut. But if we predetermine to take a tough route, then that is the route we take, weariness and pain notwithstanding.

Jesus modeled how to gain victory in times of crisis and temptation by committing ourselves to obey God's Word before *the crisis comes.* Our decision in those quiet moments clears our minds and hearts to endure and overcome. To "not decide," is to go into trials with a divided heart and during the crisis we are open to temptation and failure. Not so with Jesus. After His last prayer in Gethsemane, Jesus walked out with courage and compassion. "The hour has come. . ." Jesus said, "Rise! Let us go!" (Mark

> Jesus modeled how to gain victory in times of crisis and temptation by committing ourselves to obey God's Word *before* the crisis comes.

14:41,42). That commitment, that undivided heart became the source spring for His courage in the face of torture, and compassion in the face of brutal ignorance. Even at His

On Friday, what looked like death was really life!

betrayal, Jesus cared enough to heal the ear of an enemy (Luke 22:50,51). From that moment in Gethsemane, He submitted to cruel, sinful men and even loved them, because of His surrender to His Father (1 Peter 2:18–25).

THE EXPOSÉ

The crisis of Calvary exposed His soul. That Friday His hidden strength revealed His courage and compassion which enabled Him to love others, forgive the undeserving and uncaring — "Father forgive them." From the cross He cared for His mother's physical, emotional and spiritual needs — "John, Behold your mother." He revealed His humanity and weakness — "I am thirsty." He sang a hymn of victory even while *feeling* alone — "My God, My God, Why have You forsaken Me?" He reached out to a lost, forgettable thief and remembered him — "Today, you will be with Me in Paradise." He completed the course, finished the race, and endured the pain to secure the victory for others — "It is finished." Finally, Jesus' commitment and love lead Him to faith. Here the reverse economy of the Gospel shines through clearly. *On Friday, what looked like death was really life!* It looked like defeat, but it was victory! Jesus' last statement from the cross was one of faith and victory — "Father, into Your hands I commit My spirit."

Jesus' first three statements from the Cross came soon after His crucifixion at 9:00 A.M. His last four statements came just before His death at 3:00 P.M. Here is each of the statements and the themes on Jesus' heart those six hours that Friday.

✝ "Father Forgive Them . . ."	**Forgiveness**
✝ "Behold, Your Mother . . ."	**Family**
✝ "I Thirst" . . .	**Fragileness** [of life]
✝ "My God, Why Have You Forsaken Me?"	**Forsakenness** [unjust suffering]
✝ "Today, you will be with Me in Paradise."	**Future** [Heaven]
✝ "It Is Finished . . ."	**Finality** [the significance of the Cross]
✝ "Father, Into Your Hands I Commit My spirit."	**Faith**

James 1:3,4 says, "Count it all joy when you encounter various trials, for the testing of your faith produces endurance."

Like Jesus, our endurance to do God's will flows from our commitment in our quiet Gethsemane garden to *take up our cross and follow Jesus* before our trial comes.

REFLECTING ON LESSON ONE

1. Why does the stress of a crisis often reveal the "real you"?

2. Describe Jesus Christ's attitude during His suffering (see 1 Peter 2:18–25).

3. How could Jesus respond with compassion to His torturers?

4. How are public battles won with private decisions?

5. Describe how Calvary shows that love is not just a "feel-good action."

6. Mention three of Jesus' statements from the cross and the theme they portray.

7. Name one temptation of your life where you can "commit yourself in a garden to obey God's Word."

2

T W O

FATHER, FORGIVE THEM . . .

LUKE 23:26–37

Forgiving those who hurt us is hard. It is especially difficult to forgive the unrepentant, unloving, uncaring, unlovable, and the malicious. Yet Jesus forgave. Shakespeare wrote, "To err is human, to forgive is divine." Our culture writes, "To forgive is divine, to get even is human!"

Jesus not only forgave, He calls us to forgive too. How could He forgive those insensitive, unthinking Roman soldiers who followed orders no matter who it hurt? To understand this is our first step toward forgiving others.

"Father, forgive them . . ." deals with *the theme of Calvary* — forgiveness. Jesus' actions were living parables of forgiveness. He always told the truth "straight as a string," but no one could call Him callous, insensitive or unloving. He called divorce a sin but treated divorcees with respect and compassion (John 4:7–26). To those who misunderstood Him, He understood *them* and cared. How did He respond to the Samaritan village that refused to show Him and His followers hospitality with lodging and food? Did Jesus condemn them for their misunderstanding and prejudice? No. He forgave those who *knew not what they were doing* (Luke 9:51–56).

Likewise, Jesus prayed for the Roman soldiers from the Cross, "Jesus said, 'Father, forgive them, for they do not know what they are doing.' And they divided up his clothes by casting lots" (Luke 23:34).

FOUR THEMES OF FORGIVENESS

Jesus' statement "Father, forgive them . . ." shows us four themes of forgiveness:

✞ Forgiveness reaches out to the undeserving

✞ Forgiveness comes from God

✞ Forgiveness does not always change the forgiven

✞ The forgiven must *learn* to forgive.

FORGIVENESS REACHES OUT TO THE UNDESERVING

Jesus' words of forgiveness were directed to the Roman soldiers who had beaten Him so badly that He could not carry His own cross to Calvary. They had mocked Him with a purple robe and a crown of thorns. They had beaten Him on the face while He was blindfolded and asked Him, "Prophesy! Who hit you?" (Luke 22:64).

Little did they know that He *could* tell them who hit Him. He could even tell each of them about their deepest fears and hurts. He knew their hearts, their prejudice, their pain. They beat Him and from the Cross He blessed them.

There was no blindfold when they nailed Him to the

Cross. Surely Jesus did not respond as others they had crucified. Others responded to crucifixion by either spewing vile profanity or weeping for pity. Jesus had a calm assurance as the soldiers nailed His hands and feet. The soldiers thought Jesus' life was in their hands, but they did not know that they were crucifying the Lord of Life, Who held *their lives* in His hands. They were so undeserving but He forgave them, not because of who *they* were but because of who *He* is.

FORGIVENESS COMES FROM GOD THE FATHER

Why did Jesus ask His Heavenly Father to forgive these men, when He could have forgiven them Himself? He later forgives the repentant thief and rewards him with Paradise (Luke 23:43). Earlier He had forgiven others (Matthew 9:6; Mark 2:10). But for these soldiers Jesus asked the Father to forgive them. Why? Because *forgiveness ultimately comes from the Father.* An offense against the Son was an offense against the Father. A sin against any other person was — and is — a sin against God; like the prodigal son said to his father, "Father, I have sinned *against heaven* and against you. I am no longer worthy to be called your son" (Luke 15:21). Joseph had the same response when Potiphar's wife tried to seduce him into adultery, "My master has withheld nothing from me except you, because you are his wife. How then could I do such a wicked thing and *sin against God*?" (Genesis 39:9, emphasis added).

So the offender should seek forgiveness from both the offended and from God. Jesus modeled forgiveness from the Cross and prayed for those who had offended Him. He calls us to follow His example and "Love your enemies and pray for those who persecute you" (Matthew 5:44b). A Christian's forgiveness comes from

> Forgiveness ultimately comes from the Father.

God and the forgiveness Christians give to their enemies also *comes from our Father.*

Paul wrote in Ephesians 4:32, "Be kind and compassionate to one another, forgiving each other, *just as in Christ God forgave you*" (emphasis added). Our *vertical relationship* with

> We forgive our enemies not because they need forgiveness but because God has forgiven us.

God should control our *horizontal relationships* with others, even our enemies. *We forgive our enemies not because they need forgiveness* — though they do need it. We do not forgive others because they want forgiveness, or because they forgive us, or because they deserve forgiveness — they do not. We do not forgive others because they repent — they usually do not. We forgive them *because God has forgiven us.* Forgiven people are forgiving people. Those who have received grace are gracious people. Those who have experienced God's love are loving people. The reverse is also true: those who refuse to love, demonstrate that they do not know the love of God. "If anyone says, 'I love God,' yet hates his brother, he is a liar. For anyone who does not love his brother, whom he has seen, cannot love God, whom he has not seen" (1 John 4:20).

FORGIVENESS DOES NOT ALWAYS CHANGE THE OFFENDER

The direct recipients of Christ's forgiving words from the Cross were the Roman soldiers — some of whom may have come back to murder and pillage in and around Jerusalem in the years that followed. The Scripture never indicates any positive response by these soldiers — except for their commander who realized Christ's uniqueness. But these soldiers gambled for His clothes and seemed oblivious to His sacrifice for them. They were so caught up in the events of their lives that they missed *the event* of their lives.

Even Christians who have God's forgiveness can focus on their own hearts and become callous to others who we are called to forgive. The depth of our relationship with God portrays itself in how we forgive our enemies and offenders. Peter asked Jesus if he should forgive an offender as many as seven times. To which Jesus replied, "I tell you, not seven times, but seventy-seven times" (Matthew 18:22). Then Matthew wrote *"for this reason"* Jesus told the parable of the unforgiving servant (Matthew 18:21–35 NASB). In this parable the servant owes 10,000 silver talents which amounts to a debt of six million dollars! He could never repay it, so he begs for mercy. The master, moved with compassion, forgives the debt. The servant leaves and soon finds a fellow servant who owes him a hundred denarii which amounts to $17.00. The forgiven servant grabs the man who owes him the $17.00 and chokes him. The man begs for forgiveness — just like the servant had to his master — but the servant was unwilling to forgive and had him thrown into prison until he repaid the $17.00. The other servants told their master of this event so he had the unforgiving servant brought before him. The master then turned that servant over to be tortured until his *original debt* of $6,000,000 was repaid. Of course it could never be repaid.

Even Christians who have God's forgiveness can focus on their own hearts and become callous to others who we are called to forgive.

THE FORGIVEN MUST *LEARN TO FORGIVE*

What does this story teach? The forgiven must *learn* to forgive. Forgiving does not come naturally or easily even for a Christian. Jesus said, "For if you forgive men when they sin against you, your heavenly Father will also forgive you. But if you do not forgive men their sins, your Father will not forgive your sins" (Matthew 6:14-15).

It always costs something to forgive.

Forgiveness is never cheap. *It always costs something to forgive.* Forgiveness was not cheap for God. It cost Him something more precious than anything — the life of His own Son. Forgiveness is never cheap for us either. It is often the most expensive thing we can give.

If ever we think that the Father just casually dismisses and forgives our sins, just one look at Calvary will show us how much God hates sin and how it must be paid for with the highest price. God is serious about sin and punishes it.

The parable of the unforgiving servant shows that forgiveness will be taken away if we do not forgive. The $6,000,000 represents a debt that we cannot pay — our sins before God. Forgiveness of that debt represents salvation. The unforgiving servant had salvation. The $17.00 represents the injury that others inflict on us. When the servant would not forgive he received back his original indebtedness — his $6,000,000 debt which he could never repay. If his sins are not forgiven where does he go? To the tortures. Hell. But the unforgiving servant did not go to Hell for the $6,000,000 debt; he went over the $17.00 he refused to forgive.

What does the $17.00 debt represent to us? The grudge held against that neighbor who borrowed the power saw and returned it broken. Or, the ladder that never was returned. The dent in the new truck or car. That cutting remark. That bit of gossip.

Do we forgive others because we do not want to go to Hell for such a little price? Do we pray for God to forgive *others* because we do not want them to go to Hell over $17.00 — because "they don't even know what they are doing." That is exchanging heaven for hell over such little items.

Forgiving also means *learning* to forget. God is a forgetful God when it comes to our sins. In the New Covenant God said, "I WILL BE MERCIFUL TO THEIR INIQUITIES, AND I WILL REMEMBER THEIR SINS NO MORE" (Hebrews 8:12 NASB). God forgets our sins not because He *cannot* remember — God is ancient but He does not have Alzheimer's. Our Father *chooses* to forget. It is His active volition to push that sin out of His memory. Christians must learn to do the same. Just saying, "Well, I forgive them, but I cannot forget." What they are really saying is, "I don't want to forget."

Psalms 103:12 says, "As far as the east is from the west, so far has he removed our transgressions from us." Note that it does **not** say, "As far as the North is from the South," because you can only go so far North and then you must go South. Therefore the distance from the North Pole to South Pole is a specific distance — 12,403 miles. But when will East meet West? Never. You can go East for the rest of your life and never meet West. *How far is it from East to West? Infinite. That is how far God removes our sins from us!* Corrie ten Boom was known to say that God put our sins in the deepest sea then put up a sign that said, "No Fishing." There is *no fishing* for our own sins, nor the sins of others. Forgetting means not fishing in that deep sea.

Why does fishing out a sin or grudge make such a huge difference? Paul wrote, "Do not be deceived: God cannot be mocked. A man reaps what he sows" (Galatians 6:7). If you sow a thought, you will reap an action. If you sow an action, you will reap a habit. If you sow a habit, you will reap a character. If you sow a char-

How far is it from East to West? Infinite. That is how far God removes our sins from us!

24

acter, you will reap a destiny. You are not what you think you are: *What you think — you are!* That is why Jesus taught that *attitude* was as bad as action. Hatred equals murder. Lust equals adultery . . . (Matthew 5:22,28).

When we remember how much we have been forgiven, we will forgive those who offend us.

The unforgiving servant of Matthew 18 forgot "that he has been cleansed from his past sins" (2 Peter 1:9). *When we remember how much we have been forgiven, we will forgive those who offend us.* The forgiveness of God will flow through us to those around us. We will be the light of the world and will salt them without insulting them. We forgive others not because they deserve forgiveness, but because *we did not deserve forgiveness* and God forgave us anyway. "Be kind and compassionate to one another, forgiving each other, **just as** in Christ God forgave you" (Ephesians 4:32). Then, like Jesus, our vertical relationship with God will dictate our horizontal relationships with others.

And the forgiven will forgive.

REFLECTING ON LESSON TWO

1. Why are we to forgive the unrepentant, undeserving, and uncaring?

2. Why did Jesus ask God to forgive them — instead of forgiving them Himself?

3. How should our vertical relationship with God affect our horizontal relationships with other people, such as our family, other believers, coworkers, and enemies?

4. By what measurement does the Apostle Paul say we are to forgive others in Ephesians 4:32?

5. Mention three of the themes of forgiveness and explain them.

6. From Jesus' parable recorded in Matthew 18, why must a Christian learn to forgive even debts as little as $17.00?

7. How does forgiveness also mean forgetting?

BEHOLD, YOUR MOTHER.
BEHOLD, YOUR SON.

JOHN 19:19–27

Every mother is concerned about her son's clothes, especially when he goes out into public. Jewish moms were no different. Imagine the horror of Mary standing by the cross and looking up at her son, naked before the whole world. He hung and she stood (John 19:26). Both their hearts were torn as they looked at each other. She had such great hopes for this Son of miraculous birth.

But now He hung there with a sign above his head that read, "Jesus of Nazareth — King of the Jews." That sign was meant as a slap in the face from Pilate to the Jews. The statement "Jesus of Nazareth" instead of "Jesus son of Joseph" meant that Jesus' birth was suspect. When a Jewish boy's parents were not married nine months before his birth, the father could not claim the boy as his son — which usually happened at the age of twelve. Then the boy would be known by the name of the city where he grew up.

Thus, "Jesus of Nazareth" meant that Joseph was not His father and Pilate mocked the Jews by writing that "Your King is an illegitimate son." But Pilate and the Jews knew only part of the story. Yes, Joseph was not

Jesus' father but God Himself was Jesus' father through the virgin birth.

So Mary stood at the foot of the Cross with everyone questioning everything about Jesus including His birth, His message, His power, His Lordship. . . . Even the hope He shared with so many, now seemed hopeless. As the minutes ticked by that Friday morning Simeon's prophecy about the Baby Jesus came true: "The child's father and mother marveled at what was said about him. Then Simeon blessed them and said to Mary, his mother: 'This child is destined to cause the falling and rising of many in Israel, and to be a sign that will be spoken against, so that the thoughts of many hearts will be revealed. And *a sword will pierce your own soul* too'" (Luke 2:33–35, emphasis added).

JEWISH CLOTHES AND ROMAN GAMBLERS

The words of Jesus to Mary and John came soon after His crucifixion, just after the soldiers gambled for His tunic. Jewish men usually wore five garments: a headpiece, shoes, a robe, a girdle and an undergarment. The headpiece was a turban or a cloth to keep their hair back out of their face. The shoes were usually sandals. The outer robe was ankle length with slits up both sides and one in the top. The girdle was a belt that kept the outer robe close to the body. The undergarment was a soft tunic which was worn next to the skin and dropped to just above the knees. John — to whom part of this statement was spoken — mentions two special differences in Jesus' tunic. John calls it a "Khiton" which was the tunic of a High Priest and it was *seamless* — made from one piece (John 19:23). Someone had taken much time and care to weave this tunic for Jesus. It

Did Mary make this tunic? Did that tunic symbolize all her hopes and dreams for her Son?

28

was the Jewish custom that the mother of a son would hand-make and give a tunic to her son as he began his own adult life. *Did Mary make this tunic? Did that tunic symbolize all her hopes and dreams for her Son?* If so the actions of the Roman guards become of greater significance.

As the soldiers gambled for His tunic, Mary watched with horror.

It was Roman military tradition that five men attend crucifixions — a centurion officer and four soldiers who stood guard around the cross. One of the benefits of attending a crucifixion was that the four soldiers got the clothes of the crucified man. These men divided the outer robe of Jesus into four pieces. When they got to the seamless tunic, they realized it was much too valuable to divide and cutting it would destroy its uniqueness. Apparently each soldier determined to have "all of it or none of it." So they gambled for Jesus' tunic by throwing dice. This fulfilled David's prophecy in Psalm 22:18. We will see later in "My God, Why have you forsaken me?" that Psalm 22 fulfilled an important role for believers that Friday.

A MOTHER'S DREAMS, A SON'S VISION

As the soldiers gambled for His tunic, Mary watched with horror as they treated so coarsely the garment she took months to weave with her own hands. That tunic represented all her hopes and dreams for her Son. Even before His birth she "treasured up all these things and pondered them in her heart" (Luke 2:19). She had pondered and treasured the proclamation of the angel Gabriel and the pain of His birth — the conception was supernatural; the delivery was not. Mary treasured the words of shepherds, the prophecies in the temple about Jesus, the words of the Magi, His confounding of the

Jewish scholars at age 12, His wedding miracle, and His synagogue prophecy that "The Spirit of the Lord God is upon me . . ." (Luke 4:18–19). Then came the three and a half years of miracles and messages. And now this. One tunic containing all those dreams became a trophy to four gamblers that Friday morning. Her heart was broken. The sword had plunged.

Jesus saw. Jesus cared. Jesus spoke.

"When Jesus saw his mother there, and the disciple whom he loved standing nearby, he said to his mother, 'Dear woman, here is your son,' and to the disciple, 'Here is your mother.' From that time on, this disciple took her into his home" (John 19:26–27).

Did Jesus realize this day was coming when He met grieving parents? Is this moment why He was so focused on healing their hearts? In their eyes, did He see what His own mother would experience? Was this Friday the reason Jesus stopped the funeral in Nain and raised the only son of a widow? (Luke 7:11–17). Was the joy in that mother's heart a picture of Mary's joy? Was it a picture of His own death and bodily resurrection?

CARING FOR EARTH FROM HEAVEN

Though Jesus would rise from the dead, He would not be on earth to care for her needs as was the oldest Jewish son's family responsibility. Therefore Jesus transfers that duty to His beloved apostle, John. John became Mary's *surrogate* son. "From that time on, this disciple took her into his home" (John 19:27). There she found the assistance she needed. There John, that fiery "Son of Thunder," found a lesson in love and compassion. This surrogate responsibility accounts

Though Jesus would rise from the dead, He would not be on earth to care for her needs as was the oldest Jewish son's family responsibility.

30

for part of the transformation we see in this judgmental man (Luke 9:54) who becomes known as "the Apostle of Love" (1 John). His heart was broken at Calvary, and there Jesus called him to reach beyond his own needs and through his broken-ness to reach out to others with bro-ken hearts — especially His mother

The comments of Jesus to Mary from the cross demonstrate how important respect for our physical families must be.

Mary. John responded quickly to Jesus' request "from that hour . . ."

Notice that Jesus did not pass on this responsibility to His half-brothers. They were not believers yet (Mark 6:3, Matthew 13:53–58, John 7:1–5). It took His resurrec-tion to convince them he was really the Son of God. Later, two of Jesus' half-brothers believed in Jesus and wrote books of the New Testament — James and Jude. But on that Friday, they were not believers and Jesus calls John to be a surrogate son.

Where is Joseph in this story? The Scriptures do not tell us. We see Joseph only in Jesus' early life and never after He was twelve. We also see Joseph was a man of great faith; after all he did believe the incredible story of the virgin birth! There is no Biblical evidence that Joseph was an unbeliever. Maybe he had died. The Bible does not say.

OUR SPIRITUAL FAMILY

The comments of Jesus to Mary from the cross demonstrate how important respect for our physical families must be. Jesus was obedient to Mary and His stepfather, Joseph, even through His teen years and His twenties (Luke 2:51). Also note that Jesus' family was not a perfect fam-ily. Can you imagine growing up with Jesus as your "perfect" older brother. Mary might say, "Can't you be more like Jesus?" "But mom, you treat Him like He is perfect and never does anything wrong!" Sounds like a tough family. *But perfection is not necessary for them to be spiritual and godly families.* King David was "a man after God's own heart" but he sinned. But Christians are not called to be sinless, but to respond correctly when we sin — repentance and confession (1 John 1:7–10). David was called "a man after God's own heart" not because he did not sin, but because David knew what to do when he did sin.

These words of Jesus not only show us the importance of our physical family but it shows us the importance of our spiritual family. John was a part of the spiritual family of believers. Today we call that the church, which is *the family of God. Spiritual bonds between Christians are often stronger than physical bonds between family members.* The best bonds are both physical and spiritual. As God's family, the church can become surrogate parents and children to a culture where especially young people are crying out for deep caring relationships. The number of shattered families — whether shattered by divorce or dysfunctional relationships between parents and children — cries out for Christians to be like John and "from this hour" take people into their home. This means hospitality.

HOSPITALITY AND CHRISTIAN HOMES

Hospitality could mean inviting a single mother with five kids over for Sunday dinner, or for a holiday. It can mean reaching out to that brat in the neighborhood and befriending him or her. Maybe the reason she has such hostility is because of her family life or she is being abused. Maybe she needs a surrogate mother, not to take her in

Perfection is not necessary for them to be spiritual and godly families.

32

24 hours a day, but to provide a safe harbor from the storm of life. She may need a place where she can go and know she will be welcomed and loved no matter what (Luke 15:20). Maybe in the safe harbor of your home there will be a lighthouse, where they can find "the light of the world."

Spiritual bonds between Christians are often stronger than physical bonds between family members.

My son, Drew, invited a fellow classmate home for dinner one Friday. Though we had never met him before we found "Brian" to be a nice kid, polite and quiet. Some time after dinner Drew came and asked if Brian could spend the night. "Okay," we said, "If it's alright with his parents." It was. Following breakfast on Saturday the boys asked if Brian could stay for lunch. "Okay," we said, "If his parents give permission." They did. But we began wondering because his parents did not know us at all. That afternoon the boys asked if he could stay for dinner. Another phone call. Same answer. Saturday night Drew asked if Brian could spend the night, go to church in the morning and, of course, stay for lunch. Same answer. Same response. Sunday afternoon, "Dad, can Brian . . ." "Call his parents," I interrupted Drew, "See if Brian can stay for Youth Group tonight." He could. Finally late Sunday evening Brian went home after spending all weekend with us. We wondered about it, but we did not mind.

The next weekend was the same sequence of events. And we still had not even met his parents — that came a couple of weeks later. After a month of this Drew came to me and told me Brian wanted to be baptized to accept Jesus. "Does he know what that means?" I asked. "Yes, he does. I showed him in the Bible," Drew responded. "Well, I'll have to talk with Brian and then visit his parents to get permission first." After teaching his parents they agreed. Then later they too accepted Christ through Christian baptism. Hospitality had made an eternal difference to that one family.

But it was only months later that we learned why Brian had spent so much time in our home. He had been sexually molested by his uncle and was due to appear in court to testify. His life was a storm. He needed a surrogate family, a safe harbor, a lighthouse. He needed Jesus' love expressed through a classmate at Jr. High. When he found the safety from the storm, Brian shined his light to guide his parents in.

Hospitality of a home, became Heaven in a heart.

REFLECTING ON LESSON THREE

1. Why was Calvary a sword piercing Mary's soul?

2. What connection was there between the gambling for Jesus' tunic and His statements to Mary and John?

3. Why was Jesus called "Jesus of Nazareth" instead of Jesus son of Joseph?

4. What did Mary understand, "Behold, your son" to mean to her?

5. Why didn't Jesus give the responsibility of His mother to His half-brothers?

6. How can the hospitality of opening our homes make an eternal difference to someone?

7. List some ways Christians can bring others "into their homes."

4
F O U R

I THIRST
JOHN 19:28–30

Jesus began His ministry hungry and ended it thirsty. His hunger burned in the desert, His last thirst came on the Cross. Though those desires were physical, His greatest hunger and thirst craved righteousness for us (Matthew 5:6). That righteousness came to us through Calvary. Between His hunger and thirst He performed indescribable miracles, yet He still felt weary after a long day of ministry. He too had to sleep. He too cried. He was completely human and yet completely divine.

His third saying from the Cross shows both Christ's divinity and humanity. "Later, knowing that all was now completed, and so that the Scripture would be fulfilled, Jesus said, 'I am thirsty.' A jar of wine vinegar was there, so they soaked a sponge in it, put the sponge on a stalk of the hyssop plant, and lifted it to Jesus' lips" (John 19:28–29).

John wrote that Jesus, *knowing all things had already been accomplished*, asked for a drink. *Knowing all things* demonstrates the *Divinity* of Jesus. It portrays that He was Lord even on the Cross and that He had in His mind all the Scriptures all together and all the facts and details. But even though He was Divine, His mouth still went dry and He felt thirsty.

THE FIRST DRINK

At Calvary Jesus was offered two drinks. The first He refused. The second He requested. The second came just before 3:00 P.M. The first came just after 9:00 A.M.

"They came to a place called Golgotha (which means The Place of the Skull). There they offered Jesus wine to drink, mixed with gall; but after tasting it, he refused to drink it. When they had crucified him, they divided up his clothes by casting lots" (Matthew 27:33–35).

The Romans first offered Jesus sweet wine mixed with gall. "Gall" is poisonous liver bile. It was mixed with sweet wine and given to deaden pain of dying. A Messianic Psalm prophesied about both drinks, "I looked . . . for comforters, but I found none. They put gall in my food and gave me vinegar for my thirst" (Psalms 69:20–21).

The same Hebrew word for "gall" in Psalm 69:21, also appears as "poisoned" in Jeremiah 8:14. "For the LORD our God has doomed us to perish and given us poisoned water to drink, because we have sinned against him" (Jeremiah 8:14).

Gall was not a narcotic that people took for a high. It was a poison that numbed the senses of the victim. The guards must have thought, "We may as well poison them, they're dying anyway!" The gall dulled the senses and eventually it would kill but not quickly. The Romans wanted the condemned to suffer and linger for days. The guards gave them gall just after they hung the crucified. Maybe it was to dull the sharp pain of a prisoner's forearms and feet. When they offered it to

Jesus, He refused it. *He was unwilling to dull the pain of this experience with narcotics or poison.* He had chosen the tough road. He would faithfully and *fully endure the pain.*

JESUS ACCEPTED THE SECOND DRINK

Late in the afternoon Jesus says, "I thirst" and the Roman soldiers gave Him a drink of sour vinegar-wine mixed with water. The Roman soldiers who came from Italy to Israel's hot climate realized how sick they could get drinking the water. Jerusalem's water contained bacteria that could make them violently ill, so the soldiers mixed sour wine with local well water. "Sour wine" was wine that had passed its time and had turned into vinegar. The soldiers put it in the water hoping to kill the bacteria. This water and vinegar-wine mixture was a sort of first century Gatorade. The soldiers on duty that Friday took along this drink for themselves because they expected to sit in the hot sun at Calvary until their duty was complete. That afternoon when Jesus called, "I thirst," they took a 24-inch hyssop branch and dipped a sponge in the vinegar-wine water then lifted it too His parched lips. This small act of kindness refreshed Jesus' thirst.

Jesus' thirst showed His *humanity*. Jesus knew and suffered the simplest of human desires, needs and experiences — there were no divine exceptions even at Calvary. Through His thirst He identified with what it means to be human. How He experienced empathy with us.

He was unwilling to dull the pain of this experience with narcotics or poison.

"For we do not have a high priest who is unable to sympathize with our weaknesses, but we have one who has been tempted in every way, just as we are — yet was with-

38

out sin. Let us then approach the throne of grace with confidence, so that we may receive mercy and find grace to help us in our time of need" (Hebrews 4:15–16).

We often struggle to understand the nature of Jesus who was both God and man.

Jesus was God — therefore He *knew our needs*.

Jesus was man — therefore He *understood our needs*.

WAS JESUS HUMAN OR DIVINE? BOTH!

We often struggle to understand the nature of Jesus who was both God and man. Jesus was not half-man and half-God. Jesus was completely human and completely divine at the same time.

Jesus' mother, Mary, was a virgin and His Father was God Himself. Mary wondered how she could have a child without union with a man, so the angel explained, "The Holy Spirit will come upon you, and the power of the Most High will overshadow you. So the holy one to be born will be called the Son of God" (Luke 1:35).

One day I pondered this truth while I struggled to understand the actions of my two sons — Micaiah and Andrew. I wondered, *Whose sons are they?* Are they Carol's sons or their father's sons? Then I realized that they are each the son of *both of us*. Each is completely my son and completely her son. When one of the boys acts silly or adolescent, sometimes Carol and I tease each other by saying, "That is *your son*!" Or, when either of them is brilliant or inventive, one of us quickly declares, "Now, *that is my son*!"

Was God any different at Jesus' baptism, when His voice rang from heaven? "Now, *that is My beloved Son . . . .*"

In my sons' actions, I see traits of their father and, at

other times, traits of their mother. Yet each is 100% my son and 100% Carol's son. Was Jesus any different? He was 100% Mary's son, but does that make Him any less the Son of His Heavenly Father? No. Jesus was 100% His Father's Son — **divine** — and 100% His mother's Son — **human**.

At times in Christ's life we see both His humanity — as Mary's son — and His divinity — as His Father's Son. *It was the mother's son who forgot to tell His parents that He would be at the Temple. But it was the Father's 12-year-old son who sat and confounded the learned Pharisees.* It was the mother's son who was so tired that He slept in the back of a boat during a storm. But it was the Father's son who awoke to hush the wind and waves with just the sound of His voice. It was the mother's son who wept with tears for Lazarus' grieving sisters. But it was the Father's son who said, "Roll away the stone . . ." and called Lazarus out by name.

It was the mother's son who was tempted with power to rule all the nations of the world — without going through pain of Calvary (Luke 4:5–8). But it was the Father's son who left His Throne in Heaven to be "born in a barn." It was the mother's son who cried in the garden, "Let this cup of suffering pass from Me." But it was the Father's son who said, "Not my will but Yours be done."

> It was the mother's son who forgot to tell His parents that He would be at the Temple and the Father's son who sat and confounded the learned Pharisees.

It was the mother's son whose lifeless body was buried in a tomb. But it was the Father's son who rose from the grave on Sunday morning. It is the mother's son who, because He lived among us, knows our human weaknesses. But is the Father's son who stands at God's Throne interceding for us.

40

QUENCHING THIRST

If we were at Calvary and could have quenched Jesus' thirst, what would we have done? Would we have quenched His thirst? Do not answer too quickly, because a few days before His death Jesus gave a *test* that will tell each of us how we would have responded if we were there.

It was the mother's son whose lifeless body was buried in a tomb; the Father's son who rose from the grave on Sunday morning.

Jesus said, "For I was hungry and you gave me something to eat, *I was thirsty* and you gave me something to drink, I was a stranger and you invited me in" (Matthew 25:35, emphasis added).

Jesus continued, "The King will reply, 'I tell you the truth, whatever you did for one of *the least of these brothers of mine*, you did for me'" (Matthew 25:40, emphasis added).

Inasmuch as we meet the needs, quench the thirsts of needy people around us, we also would have met Jesus' thirst on that Friday. Sometimes we invest our time based on if the person we invite for dinner can invite us in return. But Jesus said:

> When you give a luncheon or dinner, do not invite your friends, your brothers or relatives, or your rich neighbors; if you do, they may invite you back and so you will be repaid. But when you give a banquet, invite the poor, the crippled, the lame, the blind, and you will be blessed. Although they cannot repay you, you will be repaid at the resurrection of the righteous (Luke 14:12–14).

Jesus also reminds us, "And if anyone gives even a cup of cold water to one of these little ones . . . he will certainly not lose his reward" (Matthew 10:42).

Whenever we share a "cup of cold water" with someone in need we are actually sharing it with Jesus. He said so. But He also said that if we do not help the needy around us, we are withholding help from Him (Matthew 25:42–46).

LIFE IS FRAGILE

The humanity of Jesus reminds us that life is fragile. And James affirms it, "But the one who is rich should take pride in his low position, because he will pass away like a wild flower" (James 1:10).

Physically no one will get out of this life alive (except for Christians who see His Second Coming — 1 Thessalonians 4:13–18). If medical research finds a cure for every disease, such as AIDS, cancer, brain tumors, and heart disease; something *else* will kill us. "The wages of sin is death" and we all sin. Only two things from this life will survive forever — the Word of God and people. To make our lives eternally valuable, we can invest them in these two things. Not in cars, trucks, jobs, positions, degrees, success, clothes, beauty, homes, boats, flyrods, waders, flyvests or trout fishing. Only the Word of God and people will make it out of here alive . . . invest in them.

What investment? Sometimes it is as simple as a cup of cold water.

REFLECTING ON LESSON FOUR

1. How are Jesus' Divinity and humanity both shown in John 19:28?

2. Why did the Romans give the condemned gall mixed with sweet wine?

3. Why did Jesus refuse the gall-wine mixture?

4. Why was it important for Jesus to feel thirsty? See Hebrews 4:15,16.

5. Explain how Jesus could be 100% human and 100% Divine? (I.e., 100% Mary's son and 100% Heavenly Father's son.)

6. List some ways we can share a "cup of cold water" with a hurting and needy world around us?

7. How can we invest our lives in two things of eternal value?

MY GOD, WHY HAVE YOU FORSAKEN ME?
MATTHEW 27:45–49

One day when our oldest son, Mack, was just three, we visited the pheasant cages in a remote section of a county park. Carol and I strolled from cage to cage looking at the beautiful game birds, when we realized that Mack lagged behind because he was so engrossed in the birds. We crouched in the nearby bushes and watched for his reaction to our *absence*. Several minutes later when he began glancing around for us, panic rose in his eyes because he could not find us. We *were* there, nearby, watching and ready to protect him, but he could not see us. He was not forsaken but he felt like it.

Sometimes in a crisis we feel that way about God. When we are faithful with our financial stewardship and an unexpected financial burden overtakes us, we wonder, "Where are God and His promises now?" We *feel* forsaken, but later we realize that God had never forsaken us and that He was there all along. The story called "Footprints in the Sand" strolls down that same forsaken beach. The author felt forsaken but he was not.

Jesus' fourth saying from the Cross dealt with His emotion of loneliness. Christ felt forsaken. *Someone can be in*

44

front of all the world and be all alone. At almost three o'clock Friday afternoon, Jesus realized that.

Someone can be in front of all the world and be all alone.

"From the sixth hour until the ninth hour darkness came over all the land. About the ninth hour Jesus cried out in a loud voice, "ELOI, ELOI, LAMA SABACHTHANI?" — which means, "MY GOD, MY GOD, WHY HAVE YOU FORSAKEN ME?" When some of those standing there heard this, they said, 'He's calling Elijah.' Immediately one of them ran and got a sponge. He filled it with wine vinegar, put it on a stick, and offered it to Jesus to drink. The rest said, 'Now leave him alone. Let's see if Elijah comes to save him'" (Matthew 27:45–49).

THE SIN OF THE WHOLE WORLD

The common thought about this passage is that, "God poured the sin of the world on Jesus at Calvary and God cannot be where there is sin so God *turned His back on Jesus and forsook Him.* Christ, realizing that God turned His back on Him cried out, 'My God, My God, Why have you forsaken Me?'" It is said that the reason God had to "turn His back on Jesus" was because Jesus was bearing the sin of the whole world on the Cross. And because God is holy and He cannot dwell where sin is, then He had to separate from Jesus for that time. The phrase "poured our sin into Jesus" is from Taylor's paraphrase of the Bible — the *Living Bible.* That phrase does not appear in any *translation* of the Bible.

Jesus did redeem the world's sin at Calvary, but the confusion about how that redemption took place has created a misunderstanding of the fourth saying of Jesus from the Cross. The sin of the world was not some type of black metaphysical goo that God smeared on Jesus at the Cross. Sin did not seep into His pores by osmosis so that He could become sin for us. Sin did not descend from Heaven — or rise up from Hell — as some type of black cloud and envelope Jesus. God did not inject Christ with a metaphysical needle full of the sin of the world. Roger Chambers said, "In the Bible Jesus' blood was a sacrifice offered to God, not a transfusion offered to man." (See Hebrews 9:14.)

Biblically, sin is not a characteristic of the physical nature. The teaching that sin is inherently physical comes not from the New Testament but from a priest named Augustine. In 404 A.D. he took Plato's philosophy of dual paganism — which taught that the spirit is good and the flesh is inherently evil — and mixed it with his Catholic theology. One of the teachings that came down through the centuries into Protestantism says that the flesh is inherently sinful. Sin, however, is an attitude of the soul, mind and spirit, not a wart of our liver — that surgery would reveal.

Jesus did pay for the sins of the whole world through His sacrifice on the Cross (1 John 2:2). But we often misunderstand what it means for Christ to become "sin on our behalf." Paul wrote in 2 Corinthians 5:21, "God made him who had no sin to be sin for us, so that in him we might become the righteousness of God."

> **Jesus paid for the sins of the whole world through His sacrifice on the Cross, but we often misunderstand what it means for Christ to become "sin on our behalf."**

The Bible teaches an *imputed* righteousness, not an *infused righteousness*. God does "not *reckon* their sins against them." Salvation happens in the accounting of God in His mind. We are not saved by what God does in us, we are saved by what God did for us. We are changed, but that change does not save us.

"What does the Scripture say? 'ABRAHAM BELIEVED GOD, AND IT WAS

CREDITED TO HIM AS RIGHTEOUSNESS.' . . . However, to the man who does not work but trusts God who justifies the wicked, his faith is credited as righteousness" (Romans 4:3,5, emphasis added). Abraham's faith was credited to him as righteousness and that crediting — reckoning — happened in the mind of God, where Jesus offered His redemptive blood.

> It was the Father's son who quotes the first line of the Psalm that proclaims feelings can be wrong and God's Word is our security and hope.

If sin is not a metaphysical goo smeared on Jesus at Calvary and if His blood was a sacrifice offered to God, then the Father did *not* have to separate Himself from His Son on the Cross. How could God turn His back on Jesus? Jesus *is* God. Can God turn His back on Himself? If "God cannot be anywhere there is sin" then how could Jesus be where there was sin? And why would God abandon His Son at His hour of greatest need, especially when Jesus was doing God's will and expressing God's love? When everyone else turned away from Jesus, did God the Father, too?

If God did not turn His back on Jesus, then why did Jesus quote Psalm 22:1 and cry out, "My God, my God, why have you forsaken Me?"

Jesus' cry certainly displayed His intense *feelings* of forsakenness, though He *knew* He had not been forsaken. As we saw in Chapter 4, Jesus was 100% human with all our fatigue and struggles, yet He was 100% God with all God's power and authority. This cry of Christ, again shows us both His humanity and Divinity. It was Mary's son who *felt forsaken* and cries out, "My God, Why?" but *it was the Father's son who quotes the first line of the Messianic Psalm 22 that proclaims that feelings can be wrong and God's Word is our security and hope.* This Jewish hymn shows the Messiah's feelings of forsakenness and the reality of God's victory. It was a hymn the believers at Calvary needed to sing.

Psalm 22:1; *Eloi, Eloi, Lama Sabachthani*

Why did Matthew give us the precise vocalization that Jesus uttered from the cross? Why did he give it to his readers in Hebrew and then translate it into Greek (the language of the New Testament)? It is significant every time a Biblical author uses this technique. For example, when Mark records the raising of Jairus' daughter he wrote that Jesus went into the upper room: "He took her by the hand and said to her, 'Talitha koum!' (which means, 'Little girl, I say to you, get up!')" (Mark 5:41). Through this quotation technique, Mark emphasizes that Jesus is the Lord of Life. Jesus did not need to enchant the gods with, "Raz Ma Taz, Wow Pa Now; Look at me and stand up now!" Jesus did not even have to ask His Dad if He could raise her. Jesus — the Lord of Life — simply spoke to a dead girl in words she understood and told her to "Stand up!" and her pale, cold face blushed with life!

With this phrase from the Cross, Matthew knows that the Jews near the cross and his Jewish readers would automatically recognize the statement when they heard it in Hebrew. They knew it as the first line of a song they sang in the synagogue.

The Jews may have known the Psalm by heart, just as we can quote the words of several hymns if someone says the first line. *Jesus quoted only the first line but the rest of the Psalm had great meaning to the believers.* Jesus was telling his followers that they were seeing this Psalm lived out before them that Friday.

> Jesus quoted only the first line but the rest of the Psalm had great meaning to the believers.

48

The Themes of Psalm 22

✟ **The feeling of forsakenness — vv. 1–2**

This Psalm begins with the feeling of forsakenness. David felt the sensation of God forsaking Him. But had God really forsaken King David? No. God is always faithful and nearby. But David, like us and Jesus, had to deal with that emotion and combat it with the Word of God! *The Word of God gives testimony that we can trust, but the swing of our emotions are effected by the happenstance of life.* (See 1 John 3:19–21).

> The Word of God gives testimony that we can trust, but the swing of our emotions are effected by the happenstance of life.

✟ **God will deliver me — vv. 3–5** These verses show the *knowledge* — not feeling — of God's presence.

✟ **The Cross of agony — vv. 6–8**

✟ **They accused Him — v. 8 "Let God deliver Him . . ."** was fulfilled in Luke 23:35.

✟ **Help is near . . . — v. 11** God is *near not far away!*

✟ **They cast lots for His clothes — v. 18** was fulfilled in Mark 15:24.

✟ **I'll praise Thee . . . — vv. 22–23** This is not the cry of the forsaken.

✟ **God has *not forsaken Jesus* — v. 24**

"For he has not despised or disdained the suffering of the afflicted one; he has not hidden his face from him but has listened to his cry for help" (Psalm 22:24).

"For . . . he [God] has not hidden his face from him [Jesus]" demonstrates that God did not turn His back on Jesus on the cross. The Jewish listeners could understand that emotionally they may feel like God has turned His back on Jesus and them, but what looks like defeat is victory.

✝ **Many will turn to the Lord — vv. 26,27**

✝ **God rules! — v. 28** What looks like defeat is really victory!

THE FIRST LINE . . .

Psalm 22:1 is the first line of a Messianic hymn that portrayed the feelings of forsakenness and agony, the nearness of God and the victory He will bring. *If the believers knew the Psalm they could find comfort, even hope "because they knew the chorus."*

It is no different than if I were on my deathbed and my family hears me say, "I was sinking deep in sin far from the peaceful shore very deeply stained within . . . ." Would they be fearful that I had preached all these years and now doubted my own salvation? No. They would not be fearful. On the contrary, they would rejoice. Why? Because they know the rest of the hymn.

> I was sinking deep in sin,
>   Far from the peaceful shore,
> Very deeply stained within,
>   Sinking to rise no more;
> But the Master of the sea,
>   Heard my despairing cry,
> From the water lifted me —
>   Now safe am I.
>
> Love lifted me, Love lifted me;
> When nothing else could help,
> Love lifted me.

They would rejoice because they know the chorus!

Have you ever had someone start a song that you cannot get out of your head? That Friday Jesus started a song in their heads. As Psalm 22 rolled through their minds they

> If the believers knew the Psalm they could find comfort, even hope "because they knew the chorus."

50

could have realize how it pictured their experience at Calvary, *"We feel* like God has forsaken us, but we know that He has not. We will see the victory!"

It took until Sunday, but they did see victory!

REFLECTING ON LESSON FIVE

1. Can a people feel forsaken and alone when they are not? How?

2. Could Jesus in His humanness emotionally feel forsaken when He knew that God had not forsaken Him?

3. Was the blood of Jesus a sacrifice offered to God, or a transfusion offered to mankind?

4. What should we trust, our emotions or the truth of God's Word? Why?

5. Explain how we can feel forsaken when we are not, like King David expressed in Psalm 22.

6. Show how Psalm 22 relates to Jesus' crucifixion and how verse 24 declares that Christ was not forsaken.

7. Name a hymn or Christian song that has lifted your spirits when you are down. Why does singing that song encourage you?

6
S I X

TODAY, YOU WILL BE WITH ME IN PARADISE
LUKE 23:32–43

Amidst the torrid mockery Jesus faced at Calvary, He uttered no defense but entrusted Himself to God the righteous Judge — 1 Peter 2:23. No one at Calvary spoke out to defend Jesus by crying out, "This is unfair, you have the wrong man." No one spoke out for Jesus except for a thief who in his dying moments found Christ hanging there too. And finding Christ, he who had lost everything found everything one Friday afternoon.

> Two other men, both criminals, were also led out with him to be executed. There was a written notice above him, which read: THIS IS THE KING OF THE JEWS . . . One of the criminals who hung there hurled insults at him: "Aren't you the Christ? Save yourself and us!" But the other criminal rebuked him. "Don't you fear God," he said, "since you are under the same sentence? We are punished justly, for we are getting what our deeds deserve. But this man has done nothing wrong." Then he said, "Jesus, remember me when you come into your kingdom." Jesus answered him, "I tell you the truth, today you will be with me in paradise" (Luke 23:32, 38–43).

A BAD FIRST IMPRESSION

Matthew says that *both* "robbers who were crucified with him also heaped insults on" Jesus (Matthew 27:44). That morning they had both mocked Jesus; later one got better and one got bitter. The bitterness of a crucified criminal does not surprise us, but the change at Calvary became intriguing.

What happened in that six hours to transform this condemned man from a mocker to a defender?

A CHANGE OF HEART

Maybe all that the thief knew about Jesus came from that Friday and the events there and the sign above His head, "JESUS OF NAZARETH, THE KING OF THE JEWS" (John 19:19). The events of Calvary alone convinced the Roman centurion about Jesus. Maybe it convinced the thief too.

Watching Jesus at Calvary, seeing His calm, compassionate courage beaming out of His eyes certainly could melt a heart. Hearing His tender words to foe and family and listening to His forgiving prayer for the soldiers, proclaimed His divine character to the listening thief. Even in the words of Jesus' accusers, the thief could learn Christ's message, "He saved others," "He trusts in God," "'I am the Son of God'" (Matthew 27:41–43).

Most likely the thief knew of Jesus before that Friday; he could have personally heard Jesus teach, but he certainly heard the testimony of others. Who could live in Judea, especially Jerusalem, and *not* know of Jesus of Nazareth? The teaching of Jesus was so astounding that word spread throughout the whole region. Words about Jesus the Messiah were on everyone's lips. They spoke of His teachings, His miracles. After all, He raised the dead by just the sound of His voice!

However he learned of Jesus it is certain that at his death, he saw things more clearly than ever before. That Friday his mind was uncluttered by concerns of *this* world. Circumstances had brought them together but what the Romans meant to be his death, brought him life — eternally.

THE THIEF TOOK A STAND FOR JESUS

In his life the thief had stood for all that was wrong. Now on the cross he stood for the only Good One — Jesus — when no one else did. Mary — Jesus' mother — "stood" at Calvary but she was silent. This shows her faith. Calvary crushed her heart, but she knew better than question Christ's actions or worse, to try to interfere. John the Apostle was silent too. So were the other believers at Calvary, but this condemned thief spoke out. He did not speak out to the Romans who mocked Jesus (Luke 23:36) or to the Jewish leaders (who could not cast the first stone but now cast insult upon insult — John 8:7). *It was only to the other condemned criminal that the thief spoke* (Luke 23:42). He may have felt that he could only rebuke his fellow criminal — after all, who can a condemned criminal chastise? But hearing all the others mock Jesus seemed to boil up inside him and when the other criminal started in again on Jesus, he spoke out his rebuke.

But his words were a stinging rebuke to all at Calvary, if they had "ears to hear." In his rebuke the thief proclaimed his faith in God, his repentance and confessed Jesus as innocent and the Lord of victory. Everyone at Calvary needed to do the same. Few followed his lead.

It was only to the other condemned criminal that the thief spoke.

54

The thief declared his faith in God by asking the other criminal, "Don't you fear God?" Obviously the thief did fear God and his judgment to come. He knew he needed forgiveness, mercy and grace.

The thief declared his faith in God by asking the other criminal, "Don't you fear God?"

The thief showed his repentant attitude when he said, "We are punished justly, for we are getting what our deeds deserve" (Luke 23:41). He knew his sin and the justness of his condemnation.

Then he proclaimed that Jesus was innocent and guilt free, "But this man has done nothing wrong." The thief would need some prior knowledge of Jesus to know this. Here the thief saw — maybe unknowingly — the innocent Lamb of God who takes away the sin of the world.

The thief also revealed that Jesus was *still* Lord and victor, when he turned to Jesus and asked, "Jesus, remember me when you come into your kingdom" (Luke 23:42). Watching Jesus up close convinced him that Jesus was not defeated at Calvary. He would still see His throne and rule His kingdom.

To that King, this helpless thug and outcast, asked to be remembered. Like others, this outcast came to Jesus because he had nothing to lose and everything to gain. He did not know he could gain everything. He was completely bankrupt especially of hope. He had no friends, no social status, no money, no home, no life. This was his death-day confession and plea.

He realized that Calvary was *not* the end for Jesus and if only one person remembered him, that would be enough. He did not realize just how right he was.

REMEMBER ME . . .

"Then he said, 'Jesus, *remember me* when you come into your kingdom'" (Luke 23:42, emphasis added).

This was a day when everyone wanted to forget this thief and his worthless life. He was so worthless and forgettable that the authorities deemed the world better without him. His parents, his brothers and sisters, his hometown all wanted just to forget he had ever existed. On this day he wanted to be remembered. *History did not record his name, yet Jesus did record it in the Lamb's book of life* (Revelation 21:27). And nearly 2,000 years later we are still talking about him. History forgot his name but Jesus remembered.

The thief was not asking for salvation, just to be remembered. He wanted Jesus to forget about his crimes (and his sin Hebrews 8:12), and remember *him*. Curiously, Jesus said that He calls all His "sheep by name" (John 10:3). In the garden after the resurrection, a disciple encountered Jesus and thinking He was the caretaker asked Him "where they had taken my Lord" (John 20:16). He responded with just one word, "Mary." Her name. And she knew He was alive! Jesus never forgets a name.

HOW WAS THE THIEF SAVED?

"Jesus answered him, 'I tell you the truth, today you will be with me in paradise'" (Luke 23:32,38–43).

This condemned unworthy thief found salvation at Calvary. How was he saved? Certainly not by works. It was by the grace — the free gift — of Christ. Remember that the thief and Jesus lived and died under the Old Covenant, the Jewish Covenant. It

History did not record the thief's name, yet Jesus did record it in the Lamb's book of life.

56

was still the Mosaic age ruled by the Law of Moses with all the Jewish sacrifices.

Jesus' sacrifice at Calvary was the end of the Jewish Covenant and the opening of the New Covenant (Hebrews 8:13, 9:15, 13:20). Jesus' earthly ministry was a transition time between the Covenants. Jesus lived and died under the Old Covenant but taught to prepare the disciples for the New Covenant. He gave them "new wine" for their "new wineskins" (Luke 5:37,38).

But at Calvary the New Covenant did not yet exist. It did not — could not — begin until *after* Jesus' sacrifice. His blood and resurrection is the *basis* of the whole New Covenant (Luke 22:20).

It is frequently said that the thief on the cross was not baptized. But he could have been. There is no statement of Scripture that says that he was not baptized. A tremendous number of people were baptized by John the Baptist and Jesus' disciples (Mark 1:5; Luke 7:29,30; John 3:22,23; 4:1,2). He could have been one of those who heard the preaching, was baptized, then later fell away. Remember that many disciples left Jesus after His sermon on the Bread of Life (John 6:66). But this is *speculation* to say he was baptized. That's the point, it's also speculation that he was not baptized. We should base our doctrine statements of Scripture and not on speculation. It is speculation to say he was or wasn't baptized.

The Bible is clear that Jesus was the "owner" of the forgiveness of sins (Matthew 9:6). While He was alive, Jesus could — and did — forgive anyone He wanted, just as the owner of land can give property to whomever he pleases while he is alive.

But once the "owner" dies, his land cannot be given out

unless it is according to his last will and testament. *Likewise after His death, Jesus' forgiveness must be given out according to His last will and testament* — the terms of the New Covenant. Christ's Last Will and Testament is in the New Testament as recorded in Matthew 18:19,20 and Mark 16:16. Peter, in obedience to Jesus' will and testament, preached the same in Acts 2:38.

"WITH ME IN PARADISE"

Jesus' promise to the thief teaches several things about Paradise. Jesus said, **"Today . . ."** which shows that we will be conscious after death and we do not have to sleep or wait until the Second Coming to be with Jesus. It is "Today!"

"With Me . . ." proclaims that we will be with Jesus — wherever He is, we will be also. We will not be in a waiting place. We will be with Him (2 Corinthians 5:8).

"In Paradise . . ." What is Paradise? How can we define it? Our perspective of Paradise — Heaven — varies depending on our priorities. I imagine that at the Gates we will be greeted by an angel, maybe an Archangel such as Gabriel or Michael. But the angel on duty when I arrive will likely be *Clarence* (the one who helped Jimmy Stewart in "It's A Wonderful Life"). On the tour, I'll see the twelve Pearly gates, Jasper Sea, Tree of Life (which produces a harvest of new fruit each month — Revelation 22:2), and the River of Life (which, no doubt, produces a monthly migration of salmon and steelhead, and has a fly shop that's never closed). Then Clarence and I will stroll down Gold Street past all the beautiful mansions (that make Beverly Hills look like "a hole in the wall"), and when none of them is *my* mansion, I won't be disappointed. Then we'll turn down

Silver Street and when we get to the end of all those gorgeous mansions and none is mine, I won't be disappointed. Then we'll go down to Bronze Street, none is mine. Still, no disappointment. Then we'll go down Copper Street, then Aluminum Street, then Stainless Steel, then Iron, then all the way down to Asphalt Street, then Concrete, then on to Gravel Road, then Dirt Road, then Two-Track Trail, then finally we get to a muddy, mosquito infested swamp. If Clarence shows me a Tar Paper Shack and says, "Here you are. That's yours," I won't be disappointed. Why? Because what makes Paradise, paradise to me is *not* Mansions on Gold Street, Pearly Gates, the River of Life or fruit from the Tree of Life — you can take all that stuff and throw it in the Jasper Sea. *What makes Paradise, paradise to me is being **with Jesus!*** Jesus said, "Today, you will be *with Me in Paradise.*" Any place with Jesus will be Paradise to me.

Really?

Well, when we get to Heaven just ask the thief.

> **What makes Paradise, paradise to me is being with Jesus!**

REFLECTING ON LESSON SIX

1. Explain how the repentant thief had a "change of heart" at Calvary.

2. From his rebuke of the other criminal show how the thief displayed faith, repentance and confession of Jesus' innocence. (Luke 23:39–42).

3. How did the thief's request in Luke 23:42 display his faith that death would not destroy Jesus?

4. Why do you think the thief wanted to be *remembered*?

5. What did Jesus' death have to do with the end of the Old Covenant and the beginning of the New Covenant?

6. Was the thief baptized? Should we be baptized? (see Matthew 28:18-20; Acts 2:38)

7. What will make Paradise, a paradise for you?

7

IT IS FINISHED
JOHN 19:23-30

Calvary was the end, but it was also the beginning. "It is finished" shows that the end will be the beginning. Calvary was a finish of many things, including the finish of the Old Covenant with the physical nation of Israel, the fulfillment of Old Testament prophecy and the completion of Christ's earthly ministry. But it was also the beginning. Luke opens his second book about Jesus and His followers by writing, "In my former book [the Gospel of Luke], Theophilus, I wrote about all that Jesus *began* to do and to teach until the day he was taken up to heaven, after giving instructions through the Holy Spirit to the apostles he had chosen" (Acts 1:1-2, emphasis added). Luke says that Jesus' earthly ministry was what Christ *"began to do and teach . . ."* This implies that Jesus is continuing His ministry while guiding His followers and ruling His Kingdom from Heaven. Acts is a record of what Jesus *continued* to do and teach. Calvary was an end but it was also a beginning.

The phrase that Jesus said, "It is Finished" (Greek: τετέ-λεσται — tetelestai) had twelve (12) common uses in the

61

first century. Each relates to Christ's death and adds insight to His sacrifice.

1. A task was accomplished
2. A dangerous feat was performed
3. A play was put into effect
4. Someone's will was carried out
5. A promise was fulfilled
6. Orders to a soldier were executed
7. An oath was made effective
8. A legal document was formally executed
9. A prayer was brought to pass
10. A given time period came to an end
11. A sickness reached its end
12. A debt was paid

1 — A TASK WAS ACCOMPLISHED

"'My food,' said Jesus, 'is to do the will of him who sent me and to finish his work'" (John 4:34).

Even from the age of twelve, Jesus had a passion for being about His Father's business (Luke 2:49). During His ministry Jesus responded by doing His Father's work, living His Father's actions, and presenting His Father's heart and will. Everyone knew that when you saw Jesus, you saw the Father.

Even here at His sacrifice and His death, we see that Jesus was accomplishing His Father's task to save the world. But Calvary was more than a task of an errand boy; it was *a dangerous feat* for the Man of God.

The Greek phrase *tetelestai* had twelve common uses in the first century.

62

2 — A DANGEROUS FEAT WAS PERFORMED

"The reason my Father loves me is that I lay down my life — only to take it up again. No one takes it from me, but I lay it down of my own accord. I have authority to lay it down and authority to take it up again. This command I received from my Father" (John 10:17–18).

> The sacrifice of Jesus put into effect the plan of God to call people out of darkness into His marvelous light.

In our culture a "dangerous feat" is one where a person risks death. Some dangerous feats are for no real purpose except entertainment, such as a trapeze group without a net, or a bungee jumper leaping from Royal Gorge bridge. However, a bomb squad disarming an explosive device performs a dangerous feat by risking their lives to save others. A fireman entering a burning building to rescue a baby risks his life to save the helpless.

Jesus' "dangerous feat" at Calvary was different. Yes, He did save others by His feat. Yes, He saved others who were helpless without Him: "when we were still powerless, Christ died for the ungodly" (Romans 5:6). Jesus did not just risk His life to save others, He *gave* His life to save them. When He did, it was not by coincidence, because God's *plan was put into effect.*

3 — A PLAN WAS PUT INTO EFFECT

"And he made known to us the mystery of his will . . . to bring all things in heaven and on earth together under one head, even Christ. In him we were also chosen, having been predestined according to the *plan* of him who works out everything in conformity with the purpose of his will," (Ephesians 1:9–11, emphasis added).

The sacrifice of Jesus put into effect the plan of God to call people out of darkness into His marvelous light (1 Peter 2:9). Both Ephesians Chapter 1 and Romans Chapter 8 mention that God has predestined us according to His plan. Paul writes in Romans 8:29, "For those God foreknew he also predestined to be conformed to the likeness of his Son, that he might be the firstborn among many brothers."

God did not predestine who was going to be saved but *how* they were going to be saved. They would be saved by "conforming to the likeness of His Son." That was God's plan to call people into conforming to the likeness of Christ. Jesus said essentially the same thing in John 14:6, "I am the way and the truth and the life. No one comes to the Father except through me" (John 14:6). At Calvary Jesus sealed God's plan to draw mankind into the image of His Son — that is what happens when God's *will is carried out.*

4 — SOMEONE'S WILL WAS CARRIED OUT

"Going a little farther, he fell with his face to the ground and prayed, "'My Father, if it is possible, may this cup be taken from me. Yet not as I will, but as you will'" (Matthew 26:39).

At Calvary the will of God was carried out. It was also Jesus' will. "For the Son of Man came to seek and to save what was lost" (Luke 19:10). As we mentioned earlier Jesus struggled with this decision in the Garden. *Is there any other way to fulfill this mission*? Jesus wondered. But Calvary was the Father's will. At Calvary we see the agreement made between the justice of God and the love of God. The justice of God demanded that sin must be paid for, and the love of God desired for all men to be saved. Man

> **At Calvary the will of God was carried out. It was also Jesus' will.**

64

could not save himself, so the justice of God and the love of God made a covenant at Calvary to receive the sacrifice of Jesus as redemption — payment — for the sins of the whole world (1 John 2:2). And when Jesus carried out the Father's will *a promise was fulfilled.*

From the Garden of Eden, God had promised to deliver us from our sins.

5 — A PROMISE WAS FULFILLED

"'And I will put enmity between you and the woman, and between your offspring and hers; he will crush your head, and you will strike his heel'" (Genesis 3:15).

From the Garden of Eden, God had promised to deliver us from our sins. The seed of the woman, Jesus — born of Mary — would have "His heel" struck by Satan. That was Jesus' death that Friday. But God also promised that Jesus would crush Satan's head — *that* was Jesus' resurrection on Sunday.

6 — ORDERS TO A SOLDIER WERE EXECUTED

"So Jesus said, 'When you have lifted up the Son of Man, then you will know that I am the one I claim to be and that *I do nothing on my own* but speak just what the Father has taught me'" (John 8:28). "For our struggle is . . . against the spiritual forces of evil . . ." (Ephesians 6:12).

Jesus was in a spiritual battle His whole life. Herod, motivated by Satan, tried to kill baby Jesus. Satan tempted Jesus in the desert and tried to have Him killed before His time. But Jesus was faithful to His calling as a soldier of God. As a warrior from a distant land — Heaven — Jesus was called to sacrifice His life for freedom. Freedom not for His homeland but freedom for the aliens and sojourners of this land (Ephesians 2:19 and 1 Peter 2:11).

7 — AN OATH WAS MADE EFFECTIVE

"For the wages of sin is death, but the gift of God is eternal life in Christ Jesus our Lord" (Romans 6:23).

This vow that was fulfilled at Calvary had two sides. First, Calvary proclaims that sin carries heavy wages and they must be paid. Jesus paid them. Secondly, Calvary offers a gift — eternal life.

8 — A LEGAL DOCUMENT WAS FORMALLY EXECUTED

"'This is the covenant I will make with the house of Israel after that time, declares the Lord. I will put my laws in their minds and write them on their hearts. I will be their God, and they will be my people. No longer will a man teach his neighbor, or a man his brother, saying, "Know the Lord," because they will all know me, from the least of them to the greatest. For I will forgive their wickedness and will remember their sins no more'" (Hebrews 8:10–12).

The New Covenant was so superior to the Old Covenant that the author of Hebrews calls the Old Covenant "only a shadow of the good things that are coming. . ." (Hebrews 10:1). The New Covenant is a binding agreement sealed by the blood of Christ (1 Peter 1:19,20) and sealed by the Holy Spirit in the life of a Christian (Ephesians 4:30).

9 — A PRAYER WAS BROUGHT TO PASS

"Jesus called out with a loud voice,

This vow that was fulfilled at Calvary had two sides.

66

'Father, into your hands I commit my spirit.' When he had said this, he breathed his last" (Luke 23:46).

Jesus last two statements on Calvary came moments apart. He said, "It is finished." Then, as we will see in Chapter Eight, He prayed His last prayer.

10 — A GIVEN TIME PERIOD CAME TO AN END

"Christ redeemed us from the curse of the law by becoming a curse for us, for it is written: 'Cursed is everyone who is hung on a tree'" (Galatians 3:13).

With the death of Jesus came also the end of the control of the Law on our lives. The death of Christ proclaimed the end of all that the Law was to do — to lead us to Christ (Galatians 3:23–25). Here was the fulfillment of all the Law and the Prophets, hanging on the Cross.

11 — A SICKNESS REACHED ITS END

"Since the children have flesh and blood, he too shared in their humanity so that by his death he might destroy him who holds the power of death — that is, the devil — and free those who all their lives were held in slavery by their fear of death" (Hebrews 2:14–15).

Sin is deadlier than any physical disease. Cancer, AIDS and heart attacks will never hold as much sway as sin. Death means "separation." Physical death results when the spirit separates from the body. Spiritual death occurs when our spirit is separated from God by sin. Eternal death results when a person is separated from God forever in Hell. Fortunately, there is also life. Life is union. When our spirit and body are united, we have physical life. If our spirit is united with God through Jesus we have spiritual life; and Christians will have eternal life by being united with God forever.

Someone said, "Twice born people die once, and once born people die twice."

12 — A DEBT WAS PAID

"For it is by grace you have been saved, through faith — and this not from yourselves, it is the gift of God — not by works, so that no one can boast" (Ephesians 2:8–9).

The most common usage of the phrase "It is finished" was at the top of the receipt or bill of sale. They would write "*Tetelestai*!" when the debt was "paid in full."

Our sins are like a insurmountable debt that we cannot pay. The Old Testament sacrifices did forgive sins, but not completely. They only kept the Jews from being consumed by their sins until the Messiah came to rescue them. The Old Testament sacrifices were paying the interest on that insurmountable debt that we owe — the $6,000,000 of Jesus' parable in Matthew 18. The Old Testament blood sacrifices paid the interest on the debt but could not make a dent on the principle amount of the debt. At Calvary, *Jesus paid the debt in full!*

REFLECTING ON LESSON SEVEN

1. What were some things that were "finished" at Calvary?

2. How was the Cross *not* the finish for Jesus?

3. Explain how Jesus' action at Calvary was a "dangerous feat."

4. Did God predestine *who* was going to be saved or *how* they must be saved?

5. How was Calvary the signing of a "legal document" — a covenant — between God and man?

6. What "time period came to an end" at Calvary?

7. How was Calvary "payment in full"?

FATHER, INTO YOUR HANDS I COMMIT MY SPIRIT

LUKE 23:44–49

To be "in God's hands" does not mean to have no pain, no trials and no suffering. At Calvary Jesus suffered not for His own unrighteousness. He suffered for doing good, but it was no accident. Jesus' sacrifice was His intentional surrender to God's will, for your salvation, and into their hands . . .

IN *OTHERS' HANDS*

For twelve to 18 hours before His death, Jesus was in someone else's hands other than His Father's. He could have resisted, He could have saved Himself, He could have called all of His torturers and mockers to their graves with just the whisper of His voice. But praise God, He did not.

In the Garden, Jesus would not put Himself in the hands of Peter who swung his sword to defend Jesus. Jesus rebuked Peter, because He knew the Sword of the Spirit was more powerful than any sword of Damascus steel.

Judas had taken money from the hands of the Pharisees. In the Garden, Judas' money-stained hands pulled Jesus close enough to betray Him with a kiss. It was earlier that evening that Jesus had dipped bread with His hand and handed it to Judas. Now Judas handed Jesus over to the mob.

The mob, many of which might have been fed fish and bread by Jesus' hands near the Galilean Sea, now took Jesus away with clubs, torches and swords.

During the trials of deceit and lies, the High Priests, Pilate, Herod and the Sanhedrin thought that Jesus' fate was in their hands. Unknowingly, their fate was in His hands — His soon-to-be-pierced hands. It is another paradox of the Gospel. In condemning Him they inadvertently provided the only way for their forgiveness for this horrible sin and hatred.

During the beatings, Jesus endured the pounding of Roman and Jewish hands both with fists and weapons of pain. They held and bound His hands, *the hands* that had touched so many in pain and healed them all. There were the blind, the sick, the demon-possessed, the deaf, the hungry, the lonely, the grieving and the dead, and His hands had healed them. Now His hands were bound and He was beaten.

Judas dies by his own hand, not knowing that the hands of Jesus would soon be stretched out to save even His betrayer from death.

On the road to Calvary, the hands of Jesus that had carried so much wood as a carpenter's Son and had healed the lame, could not handle the weight of His own cross. Simeon of Cyrene carried it for Him. At Calvary, Roman hands stripped Jesus naked then placed Him on hand-hewn timbers, and nailed Him there. Those same Romans hands then gambled for His clothes as His mother watched.

71

"The centurion, seeing what had happened, praised God and said, 'Surely this was a righteous man.' When all the people who had gathered to witness this sight saw what took place, *they beat their breasts and went away*" (Luke 23:47,48). NASB says, "the multitudes beat their breasts . . ." Amazingly, it was not only His disciples who were distraught; it was the crowd in general. They began beating themselves on the chest with their hands.

GOD'S HANDS . . .

God was not silent during this time of trial. He displayed Himself by tearing and shaking the world with His hands (Matthew 27:51–53). By the hand of God the Temple Veil was torn in two from top to bottom. The three-inch-thick Temple Veil was laid over a pole between the Holy Place and the Most Holy Place and draped to the floor on both sides. It represented the division between God and man, but once Jesus died God tore the Veil and declared the way opened to Him because Jesus had destroyed the division — sin. God's hand covered the sun causing darkness to fall from Noon to 3:00 P.M. (Luke 23:44,45). God's hand also caused a violent earthquake and even split rocks. When He split the rocks, the tombs of recently dead saints were opened and the "raised" saints visited many in Jerusalem as a proclamation that Jesus had conquered death (Matthew 27:53; Hebrews 2:14,15).

> God was not silent during this time of trial. He displayed Himself by tearing and shaking the world with His hands.

I COMMIT MY SPIRIT . . .

"Jesus called out with a loud voice, 'Father, into your hands I commit my spirit.' When he had said this, he breathed his last" (Luke 23:46).

Jesus' last statement from the Cross was one of faith in God. As we have seen it is not in opposition to His earlier statement of "My God, My God, Why have You forsaken me?" At that time Jesus was wrestling with the emotional sensation of forsaken-

Jesus' last
statement
from the Cross
was one of
faith in God.

ness while He knew that God had not forsaken Him. Now this closing statement from Jesus seems so natural. *Gone is the anxiety of future pain that He wrestled with in the Garden. Gone is that sense of forsakenness.* Here is faith, assurance and confidence that God will receive Him and His sacrifice for our sins. Here is faith that victory is assured.

The word "commit" that Jesus used describes trust such as putting a deposit in a Bank & *Trust* Company. It carries the implication that we put ourselves "on deposit with God while trusting that He will care for us."

This last statement of Jesus from the Cross is also traditionally the first prayer that a Jewish mother teaches her son. It comes from Psalms 31:5, "Into your hands I commit my spirit; redeem me, O Lord, the God of truth." The rest of Psalm 31 applies to Christ's faith at Calvary, as well as our response to God. Psalm 31:12–13 speaks of the anguish of Calvary, "I am forgotten by them as though I were dead; I have become like broken pottery. For I hear the slander of many; there is terror on every side; they conspire against me and plot to take my life."

Psalm 31:14–15 speaks of Christ's assurance, "But I trust in you, O Lord; I say, 'You are my God.' My times are in your hands; deliver me from my enemies and from those who pursue me."

Psalms 31:20–21 illuminates Christ's faith at Calvary, "In the shelter of your presence you hide them from the intrigues of men; in your dwelling you keep them safe from accusing tongues. Praise be to the LORD, for he showed his wonderful love to me when I was in a besieged city."

JOE AND NIC — UNLIKELY HEROES

And after these things Joseph of Arimathea, being a disciple of Jesus, but a secret one, for fear of the Jews, asked Pilate that he might take away the body of Jesus; and Pilate granted permission. He came therefore, and took away His body. And Nicodemus came also, who had first come to Him by night; bringing a mixture of myrrh and aloes, about a hundred pounds weight. And so they took the body of Jesus, and bound it in linen wrappings with the spices, as is the burial custom of the Jews. Now in the place where He was crucified there was a garden; and in the garden a new tomb, in which no one had yet been laid. Therefore on account of the Jewish day of preparation, because the tomb was nearby, they laid Jesus there (John 19:38–42, NASB).

At the trials of Jesus, Joseph and Nicodemus must have felt that their hands were tied. They had seen the Sanhedrin in this bloodletting mood before. How could they persuade the whole rabid Rabbi council? Maybe they could not have stopped them, but they could have at least spoken out. Or, tried to defend Jesus. Or, tried to do something. Anything would have been better than doing nothing. But they did nothing.

Maybe they were surprised at Jesus' lack of response to the ridiculous accusations. They may have thought He would stop this incredible travesty.

Gone is the anxiety of future pain that He wrestled with in the Garden. Gone is that sense of forsakenness.

Joseph of Arimathea and Nicodemus are heroes of the Calvary story. When no one else was willing to take a stand for Jesus these two did. The multitudes flocked to Jesus when they had nothing to lose and everything to gain. The outcasts

74

pressed around Jesus because they had no social status to lose, no friends to lose, no prestige to lose; and Jesus offered them healing, food and hope. *Joseph and Nicodemus identified with Jesus when they had everything to lose and nothing to gain.* The only thing Jesus offered them was to identify with His death. For Joe and Nic that was enough. It was all that mattered.

> Joseph and Nicodemus identified with Jesus when they had everything to lose and nothing to gain.

Because they touched His dead body with their hands, they were cursed by the Mosaic Law and forbidden to participate in the *Most Holy Sabbath.* They were forbidden to go to the Temple for public worship, to offer any sacrifices, and to share in the meals with their families. For all the Passover time they were practically in exile. Imagine not being able to be with your family or to go to church during Christmas, Thanksgiving and Easter. It would be like a preacher — who being quarantined because of a contagious disease — could not worship or preach at church on Resurrection Sunday. That is what touching Jesus meant to Joseph and Nicodemus. But it meant more. To the Jews the keeping of the Passover was the major aspect of attaining righteousness through the Law. But Nicodemus and Joseph disregarded the pseudo-righteousness of the Jewish traditions and like Paul, "counted them as rubbish" compared to the identifying with the death of Jesus (Philippians 3:1–8). To these two that Friday nothing else mattered, but to handle Jesus, and carefully wrap His body with spices and linen.

Unknowingly by identifying with His death they were also identifying with His resurrection. That was Friday, but Sunday was coming. Paul demonstrates how people today can identify with Christ's death *and* resurrection:

Or don't you know that all of us who were baptized into Christ Jesus were baptized into his death? We were therefore buried with him through baptism into death in order that, just as Christ was raised from the dead through the glory of the Father, we too may live a new life. If we have been united with him like this in his death, we will certainly also be united with him in his resurrection (Romans 6:3–5).

CARRYING ON HIS MISSION

How can we carry on His mission today? By taking up His cross and exchanging burdens with Jesus. "Come to me, all you who are weary and burdened, and I will give you rest. Take my yoke upon you and learn from me, for I am gentle and humble in heart, and you will find rest for your souls. For my yoke is easy and my burden is light" (Matthew 11:28–30).

When we surrender to Jesus we do not just give our unbearable burden of sin to Him; we exchange burdens with Christ. He forgives our sin and in turn we receive His "easy and light" burden. What was His burden? "To seek and save the lost" (Luke 19:10).

"TAKE UP YOUR CROSS DAILY AND FOLLOW ME"

"Then he said to them all: 'If anyone would come after me, he must deny himself and take up his cross daily and follow me'" (Luke 9:23). What does it mean to carry His cross? Let's examine it by reviewing the seven statements He gave at Calvary.

How can we carry on His mission today? By taking up His cross and exchanging burdens with Jesus.

76

"Father, Forgive Them . . ."

✝ Forgive and forget the sins of others against you especially our debtors and enemies . . . Even as little as $17.00.

"Mother, Behold Your Son . . ."

✝ Become a surrogate parent, brother, sister to someone in need. Become a *Christian* big-brother or big-sister.

"I Thirst . . ."

✝ Help strangers, serve others even with "a cup of cold water . . ." maybe for example to serve in a soup kitchen.

"My God, Why?"

✝ Trust God and His Word when we feel forsaken. Trust Biblical promises over our emotions.

"Remember Me . . ."

✝ Share God's grace and Gospel with the forgotten of your community. Work at the homeless shelter or with the minorities in your area.

"It Is Finished . . ."

✝ Show the courage to finish God's will for you no matter what the personal sacrifice. Keep serving and helping even when you do not feel like it.

"Father, Into Your Hands . . ."

✝ Show others Christ's love with your hands. Ask "What would Jesus do in this situation?" Study His Word to find the answer.

At Calvary God the Father received Christ's Spirit. Joe and Nic received His body. Who will with their hands take up His cross and mission?

Only those *touched* by Calvary.

REFLECTING ON LESSON EIGHT

1. How was Jesus in *other* people's hands at Calvary?

2. What supernatural events surrounded the crucifixion?

3. What does "I commit . . ." mean?

4. How does Psalm 31 enrich your understanding of Christ's last prayer?

5. Why were Joe and Nic's efforts so heroic?

6. How can we "take up our cross daily" and follow Him?

7. How can we "continue Christ's mission" today?